Discontinued Township Roads

Discontinued Township Roads

Poems by Abby Chew

Word Poetry

"Storm" originally appeared in *The Los Angeles Review*.

Published by Word Poetry
P.O. Box 541106
Cincinnati, OH 45254-1106

ISBN: 9781625490599
LCCN: 2013954949

Poetry Editor: Kevin Walzer
Business Editor: Lori Jareo

Visit us on the web at www.wordpoetrybooks.com

Acknowledgements

I am grateful to the family, friends, teachers, poets, land, and good dogs who helped these poems grow.

Deb & Dale, Emily & Ryan, Ed & Kris. Mary Birnell, Elizabeth Chew.

Dan Bailey, Barbara Bean, Courtenay Bouvier; Ian, Colin, and Clare Cheney; Brian and Marilyn Cheney, Tom Chiarella, Lisa Cooper, Curt Ellis, Carol Emery, Bill & Gigi Fenlon, David Field, Jim Galvin, Matt Gilchrist, K. Hall, Bob Hass, Wade Hazel, Joe Heithaus, Maurice Manning, Tracy Miller, Pilla Ling, Cythia O'Dell, Promise Partner, Tavia Pigg, Kieth Puckett, Hannah Reed, Matt Reynolds, Roger Reynolds, Tyler Sage, Greg Schwipps, Emily Stanley, Steve Timm, Barbara Fields Timm, Deb West, Emily Wilson, Aaron Woolf, Dean Young, Jan Zenisek.

And to all my little ones: Gus & Walt. Hannah & Quinn. Alia, Emma, & Xander.

For Don.

TABLE OF CONTENTS

I.

II.

I.

And it comes back with the odor
of the river, some way I know the lonely sources
of despair break down from too much love.

— Richard Hugo
from "The River Now"

A Girl's Story

On the south bank of Jack's Defeat Creek
I caught my first channel cat,
first largemouth bass. Years ago, I found
fresh water mussels there. Saw
my first coyote, a mother with two pups
trailing after. The wind
shrugged in from the north
or she would have scented me first.
I saw, I swear, a badger down there
the year my grandmother died.
What a vicious thing.
Just south of Tory's Run an AutoCar
sits rusting its doghouse clean through —
I saw hellbenders breeding, the eggs a mass
bigger than my fist. My god, I am struck
down by the beauty of this creek.
I have seen along its banks
animals bigger even than my dream
of you walking toward me out of the dark.

ROOFTOP

Sister learns to play harmonica
so the bats come swooping
down to meet her. The high C brings
them from their hunting.
Late in March, late at night,
she crawls out on the porch roof
to sigh and breathe them in.
They fly like flapping black gloves
when she reaches out her left hand,
hoping she might become
part of the way the movement
moves. She is not afraid of a bat
in her hair. She raises
and lowers her chin, letting the air
sift through her, in and out
with force. Come here, she says.
Come here and listen.

Snake Spring

This should work:
      1) Dig.
      2) Water comes welling.

But I tried that. No thread
bubbled up inside the hole.

If Brother was right about the Earth's blood,
creeks and rivers and such as that,
where was the scab today?

He knew where to find
morels under the lightning struck maple.

The Earth doesn't bleed the way we do.
It's a different skin.
I like knowing — blood flows all ways.

South Pasture

Seven. Riding out early
with Brother to check cows,
I held tight to his white shirt.

I kept my eye on his neck, freckles
dotted along his collar. The rise
of spine into neck into skull.

Byro grazed at the South Fork. We ate
sandwiches and drank
straight from the spring.

I woke to a low sun.
The wind picked up. My own shirt
blew tight against my back.

But I heard Byro stepping through the shallows.
Brother glowed white against the sky
where he stood listening for bawling heifers.

CO RD 950 S

Drought equals dust.
The girl wants her hair
out of her face. The boy
wings rocks
toward the South Pasture fence.
The stones bounce,
skip across land so dry
the puff of dust
rises and cannot settle.
They walk
down the brown ribbon
of Jack's Defeat looking
for empty crawdad shells.
They cross the bridge,
stand at the strip of black tar
where they have seen men
come and go on horseback,
in trucks, on foot —
carrying a bag or nothing at all
across their backs.
These two kneel
at the road's edge,
fingers to the shoulder.
They look east and west.
They look through that glimmer
for someone new on the road.
And the road is a ribbon
itself now. Even wider
than the creek and never turning.

DOGHOUSE

In summer, the dog lies
against the side
of his house in the trench
he dug there. He pretends
it's snowing. Yes —
he can pretend. He can pretend
as easily as he can love you.
As easily as he chased off
that tinker sneaking
eggs from the chicken coop, as easily
as he fought that bobcat.

Father knew it, and so he built
the house with the good roof,
thick walls. He elevated the floor
so it would not rot.
He painted the dog's name in green.
He took every care for the dog,
who is old now, and dying.

POND

In deep January I go out late. I'm not sure
how long the ice has locked itself over the pond —
I forgot to mark it. Not that it matters.
We've got six inches at least. Plenty enough to creep out,
auger a hole through the blue slab, drop
a line. It is plenty.

I will wait for the tug, fling bluegill,
wide and shining, onto the white. I will fill a bucket
with their red gills, their strings of gut.

There's a place here where I can see their heat.

SUGAR SHACK

When the nights freeze and the mornings thaw
turkey vultures come back to our ridge.
They arch and bow on fenceposts,
in the tops of raggedy pines.
Their bleak humped backs bring spring,
tangled and bright, but slow.
We tap sugar maples, hang buckets.
We catch a little blood that's not
our own for once. Somehow, this chore rests lighter
than the rest despite the burden.
At the fire, I'll become my own rotisserie, turning
to heat my shin bones, my tail bone,
all the while an eye on our sap that it might
turn thick and golden, boil itself into something sweet.
I wish the fire could do that to me. I wish
it could turn my blood, my brain, my self
into something richer and darker and better than before.

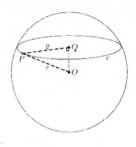

A plane intersecting a sphere
at more than one point
determines a circle.

CORNFIELD

My hair hits my belt now.
I wrap it all
around my neck to see
what fur is. Walking
the cornrows, I try
and multiply the ears.
How many kernels
live here? Everything
has a home. If I walk
right, the blades don't even
brush my arms.
The world is made
of circles, but our field
cuts straight. Daddy
planned it that way,
marked it off. All of it. Acres.
And Brother drove the plow.

OUTHOUSE

The full moon lets her use the outhouse
at night — she can check for coons and rats
when she kicks open the door. But she cannot
see the copper heads curling down in the darkness.

KITCHEN

Waving his hands, Daddy told a story. He sang a song
about the red fox stealing the old, gray goose.

And then the old gray woman
jumped out of bed, calling:

*John! John! The gray goose is gone
and the fox is on the town-o!*

I asked what happened to the goose.
Brother said, "They ate it up."

We all ate dinner real slow.

BACK TWO

Jog down this road and you won't see the culvert
once spattered with blood where our dog
killed a ground hog. You might, if you jog in late fall or winter
when blackberry brambles and cinnamon fern
die back, see the skeletons of three deer —
big bucks, not much antlered — poached and left to rot.
Now their bones lie bare in the dirt.

I stepped knee-deep into the belly of one when I jumped
down the hillside in search of morels. Granted,
I wasn't moving slow at all. I did not have an eye out
for elm and ash. I wasn't kneeling.
But the rain had brought out the green and I wanted it.
So I jumped. The stink and the slap of flesh,
the sudden buzz of flies tapping my half-closed eyes.
That kind of landing can ruin you, I know for sure.

CHICKEN COOP

When building a chicken coop, you need to know,
while your hens are stupid, unbelievably so,
they have a hunger for land and light.

Sister has a nanny goat whose legs she ties for milking.
But the chickens don't peck
at her small hands pressing beneath their feathers
for eggs. The hens let her do
the thing quietly. Of course their brains
are peanuts. Of course. But you
need to know how to frame their house.

Make it warm. Make it tight. Maybe
paint it yellow. Heat the water
in January, when you think your own fingers
may shatter from wind. Don't tell
them where you're going when you leave.
Feed on a schedule. Don't kick at the rooster
where he waits in the bare yard, aiming his nail
of a beak at your knees. Talk to them

like you do your good dog.
Tell them you are sorry. Tell them
everything you know you should.

SWINE BARN

But the pigs are Daddy's and we all know it.
They hear him coming from afar off, when he breathes
deep and says, "Smells like money!"
They grunt and grunt.
We hear them all the way up to the chicken yard.
I reckon they sing for him and Brother
says maybe. If hogs can sing.

If any ever could, these do.

Daddy knows each black and white barrel body.
He knows when they're feeling silly with wind and sun.
He sees that sow rub her spine against the split-rail,
leans to scratch her back a while.

But I've been chased by a sow, threw myself against the trough,
all that black mud. I watch them press and press each other.
Walking home from school, just as we cross our bridge,
the first drift of pig shit stench slaps across our faces.
It sits right there, waits for us to come back. It knows we will.

Sister's Night Walk

Her nightgown, white and long,
breaks the dark like a ship's prow,
then lets the night come together again
around the flitting hem.
Her breath shags out — just as white, just as white
as the cotton — from her mouth only to drift
back, curl over her ears, and away.
As she moves, her body lights up
the night for brief moments that seem like praise,
the air around her skin flaring up — auroras
drawing movement from her blood, taking
something for their own. And the night wonders
just as much: Where does she go?
What calls to draw her warm, curled body
out of the bed, into the night? Sister keeps her secrets.
If the night knows, if it holds the secret —
what waits outside the house, the porch, the gravel lane —
If the night knows, it isn't telling either.

II.

I am the self of my former shadow.
There's a forest lost in me.
When I walk there the wind scrapes overhead
Like a river I'm at the bottom of.

— James Galvin
from "Left-Handed Poem"

STORM

No one asks for silence this morning
but we give it without question. The dawn,
long past, brought a haze of heat, laid it down
over us heavy, not at all like your body
over mine. Not at all like that.
Last night, a storm struck us down.
I watched lightning crack the side of the barn,
wind snap the bean trellis, toss it up, spinning.
We salvage what we can.
The sky doesn't ask if we want our arms
slick with sweat as we pick beans, row on row,
does not ask if we want to kneel in the shade
panting like old house cats, to vomit into the weeds.
July doesn't ask what we desire.
It only creeps up over the hill each morning,
brings us what we deserve.

FERN CLIFF

Brother knows how to pull his own self up.
He's got the arms for it, long bands
of muscle. Then he turns to pull
me up, wraps his hand around my wrist
while I scrabble my feet for a hold.
He says, "Don't look down,"
when he leaps the gap from one
cliff to the next edge. I get a running start.
I see his face tense when I do it,
sail out over the sheer lip.
But I make it. I make it.

And we go.
We chase deer.
I can see into the heat of trees.
I know where my next step
will fall. And I keep up with Brother.
I stay right up. I match him step for step.

BEDROOM

At some point, Daddy stopped
letting them sleep in the same room.
Sister had made tents with her quilt
stretched between Brother's bed and desk –
they'd hunted elk,
fished for tuna in the river
rolling past the footboard.
This night, they slept hard.
Brother's arm thrown
over the side of the bed, and Sister,
Sister curled at the footboard under an afghan,
she dreamed of a new pattern
spread over the roof of the house just so.

Daddy had never jerked them by their arms.
He had whipped them with a belt,
cut a switch that time they busted
rotten eggs in the spring house. This, though,
this was different. He came through door
big as a bear, bringing a new smell, wood-rot and honey,
on his clothes when he lifted Sister from the bed.
He did not let the afghan fall, he did not pick up
the stuffed elephant she dropped at his feet.
"You're too old," Daddy said, "for this."

TOOL SHED

Daddy:

Band Saw	=	Watch your fingers
Awl	=	Settle down
Rake	=	Wear some gloves
Sawhorse	=	Hold this steady
Grain Shovel	=	Toss & Flip
Tile Spade	=	Step & Slice
Watch It	=	You get one more chance
Son of a Bitch	=	Can't nobody do anything right

Brother:

Give it	=	My hands are bigger
Don't	=	You couldn't if you tried
Stop It	=	Maybe you better go on in
Here	=	I'll let you if you don't tell Dad

COUGHING

Not lungs, this pair — they're red with bleeding now.
He spits a fine sweet mist of broken lung
across the basin. Stains the porcelain
a red I've seen before — sweet mouth of crow

untouched and cawing from a fence in fall,
his beak the red extreme of health in raw.
My Father seems a bird these days, his neck
stretched out in mornings, pressed against the haul

of lung through throat and out into the sink.
Where does a bird lift off when dying slow?
There is no action in the wait. We all wait.
We waste. We sit. We flinch. We try to sing.

We listen, tune our ears to birds again.
I'm here with Brother. Standing, pair of helmsmen.

Under the Porch

When the possum moved in
under the porch, Daddy
got the .22 and a rake
from the tool shed.
He killed that old thing, stretched
the hide on the barn to dry.

DITCH

Knee-deep in silt water, the mud formed
a second, cracking skin over our arms.
We could barely stand. Then Daddy pointed
his shovel handle to the sky, and we saw
thunderheads rolling in over the barn.

WIRE

Think about wire.
The way a barb
will catch your cuff,
your wrist, sink
its point
this deep
— rip a shred
of white skin.
Or the way
bailing wire will snap
its whip
back at you. It might
punch a hole
straight through your lip.
You might lose an eye.

MEADOW

It was just falling light
when Sister opened the door.

This was later, after her father died,
after Brother was off shoeing horses,
owned his own livery stable.
This was after she slept
with a dark-headed boy
in her bed, when she was sixteen, Daddy
gone to help Drake with a heifer
birthing her first calf, Brother sleeping
for all he was worth in his own room,
the dark-headed boy
pressing his face to her shoulder, into her hair.

But this was after all that.

This was a man
standing on her father's porch,
leaning in the doorway, pulling
off his boots with the cricket jack,
sitting at the kitchen table with a coffee mug.

Sister looked at her own hands,
red with oven-heat, looked
at the stew on the stove. She hadn't
been hungrier in all her life.

OLD AUGUSTA ROAD

Today is the Cooper's Hawk
with its fractured little chest.
The sharp-shinned hawk
lurking at the finch feeder. The Merlin
hauling the squirrel around the bend
on King's Hill.
Today is the bird you wished for
but never saw. Today
is the turkey vulture
heralding the sun's rise, lifting
her wings in salute to a new pain.
We herald the hours. We lift our faces.
We turn and fight and face it.

PEAS

Here is the prettiest plate of peas
I've ever seen. A plate so sheer
its edges fade into light.
The peas themselves placed with an eye
for perfect green-ness. It must have been
a great joy to roll each one
onto the plate and set the plate
just so on the table, left of the steak,
right of halved baked potato.
If I could do a thing with such care
maybe my kitchen would beam
with that lemon smell my mother
always managed — the rind and the pulp
floating up together from the tile,
turning out to us with every bent hinge.
That was the kitchen with the hole
in the floor where mice got in in winter,
but Daddy caught them in saucers of glue,
drowned them in five gallon buckets.
Maybe I could take the time
and grow each pea before I ate it,
before I set it on the plate with the other
perfect peas. We would all gather at the table,
wearing new clothes, made of linen, or maybe
something like wool but not so scratchy,
forks in hand. What would we be doing?
We could gather at the table again, this time

wearing our jeans and t-shirts,
this time who we are on days
when our tables are set with what peas
we could salvage from that early frost,
potato casserole and the lumpy bread
Grandma made and that big jug of sun tea.
Wouldn't that be better? Wouldn't you kill
for a glass of that tea? You could have a lemon in it.
You could sit back and roll a cigarette.
You could drink tea and listen
all day, sitting in that kitchen.

Brother Speaks from His Loft

Think about the pasture.
The rabbit warren
not quite bricked up,
escape tunnels pocking
the hill by US 40.
Think about the rabbits:
long teeth, BB eyes, the damp
fur between their nails.
Maybe you can
shoot them
with that old .22 —
it's in the hayloft,
wrapped up
in old burlap.
I hid it there.
You'll have to file
some rust away, oil things up.
But you have a steady eye.
I think we can do this thing.
The sun's just past zenith
and I know
where you hid the shells.

BRIDGE

When Brother finished rasping shingles,
he stripped off his blue shirt and climbed
up the rail at the bridge. He stood
there until the heat and the light
hurt inside his head. And he leapt.
He leapt high, and Sister saw the trees
and the sun between his rising body
and waiting water.

CALVING SHED

Brother tells Sister this story:
When Mother was here she ran the house
solid and sharp. There was lace sometimes,
tatted late at night, and floors glowing
bright when the sun lit the dust
bloating through the east windows.
Papa carried Brother in from the barn
some mornings — he remembers the height,
their monstrous shadow cast
across that golden floor. She waited
with bacon and johnny cakes. She smiled.
But that's all Brother says. Sister hasn't got
a single damn memory of any of it.
She's not sure she was even born.

HOME PASTURE

I take Byro to the home pasture
when Daddy and Brother
traipse off to fish the stock pond.
There is no other horse for me.
I drop the reins, look the old dude
in one wet, black eye, and walk away.
When he lifts his white nose
to follow, I stop. We work for hours.
The dog was easier, something about size,
about me kneeling to rub his belly.
But Byro listens hard, tries
and tries, until he knows
what I am saying with my hands.
We're done, I tell him. I smack
the column of muscle in is his neck.
He pushes his block of a head
against my shoulder. There is the soft
press of his nose against my ear.
There is the circle of his cheek
so close to my own. I can see
how his face is made.
I push my fingers through his forelock,
over the shelf of his eyes.
I say, You are beautiful.
His ears swivel. He listens even harder.

Haymow

Brother thought of a potato
in the tailpipe. He brought sister to the haymow
to see a sight. They knelt with their eyes
to chinks, waited for Daddy to fire the engine.

He came, tucking blue shirt into blue trousers, stopped
short of hauling himself to the seat.
He lifted his sharp chin. Scratched his elbow.

Sister held her breath. Brother opened his mouth.
Daddy looked all around, pressed his fingers to his temple.
He saw how the blue the sky burned. The barn door
needed painted. The gutter hung crooked on one corner.

He hollered for the boy, who was old
enough, Daddy said, to drive that tractor his own self.

THEN SHE SAYS

When they let me drive the Ford home from the cornfield,
I want it to rain. I want to see the way mist breathes itself
in from the west trees. I want to hear the tap-tap on the
tractor hood. I want the cold wind lifting its way into my
hair and touching my skull. And I want the gel of engine
heat drifting across my face. My shirt sticking to my back,
the tires spitting up clots behind. I want the thunder
murmuring, the sun fading because it can't keep up. I
want the birds chattering as they head off, to the trees, to
the caves, to the mountains: wherever it is they go. I want
the way the pole barn, from this distance, in the wet air, is
somehow holy. And I want my father and brother to see
the way the wind and the light bring the rain. They are
coming, I know, walking the edge of the field. Walking
their wide walk — their bones must be built that same way.
But Daddy has black hair, and Brother red, and mine is
yellow. I don't know if anyone understands how we're put
together. But we are. We're put together inside our bones,
and we're put together with each other, in this place.

III.

It is everything, the wet green stalk of the field
On the other side of the road.

      — James Wright
      from "Small Frogs Killed On The Highway"

Yoke

The dirt wasn't like this in Indiana,
where my brother and I dug holes
for night-crawlers, holes in red clay
that needed all the help
it could get to make all that corn.
Now, living in Iowa,
even the soil I kick back
from the edges of my driveway
blacks my boots. It's rich out here.
My brother helped birth twin
oxen calves last spring.
Their black noses pressed to my palms
like I could offer them
anything but grain
from an old coffee can.
They were leggy and light
for the one time in their lives. My brother
named them Poncho and Lefty, raised them up
to the yoke. More than 25 million days
to plough the farmland here. Still —
their noses. The thin hide
above their ankles. It's work we learn,
more than anything, and work
we teach. It's the changing
of calves into ploughshares,
prairie into furrows. It's a soil
so fertile we can't help but bend it.
And my brother, working at the forge
with a broken calabash hook, will tell you oxen
aren't built to pull. They haven't the shoulders,
the muscled legs. But they're built

to keep walking, keep working
with a yoke strapped to their horns,
keep edging that plough
through God knows how much prairie,
until we let them stop.

GARDEN

We're never sure where to start —
the snap beans seem endless.
We've tied tomatoes to stakes —
they can't make it on their own.
We hoed sweet corn all morning
long. No one knows what will survive.
We toted buckets from the creek.
By dusk, a brown bag of slug worms
slumped at the end of each row.
We wanted baths. We wanted dinner.
But now, with the silver bowl
of beans between us, we look
back from the porch. Something
in the smell of the linen of night
makes us want to start again.

BELMONT COUNTY
for M

I saw geese falling silently onto Livesy Lake. I saw the wind
braid chicory and wool grass along the shore, then whip
up the hillside to break the elm behind our house.
Running along Sandy Ridge, Brother saw a Clydesdale mare
give birth in the black dawn. He saw the foal's first steps.
We caught a broken-winged falcon on that same road,
and Brother cradled the bundled bird on his lap
the whole drive home. Months later, he stood on the ridge
at Towe Ranch, saw the sun set over this place, its blood red light
throwing shadows fifty feet long or more. Light can do that,
stretch us out into something more than our own little selves.

Daddy saw an eight-point buck, shot him poorly, tracked
two miles through the woods to the tree where he panted
and one more arrow took him down to stay.
I saw a large-mouth bass leap for a damselfly. I witnessed
the full moon corona, and when I first took my nephew
to the goat shed he fed red berry sumac to the kids,
saw their white faces turn purple with that small feast.
Each morning we see the sun rise, the pond
turn its mirror from silver to dark again. We see
each little seed thrust its head up and turn to light.
It is the dark green of our farm
in late spring that turns my heart most.
And the deep silence of early morning.

I have seen the cows in early evening, their wide, sweet faces
turned toward home, toward the barn, where Daddy waits,
the feed bucket pulling his shoulders sore from tamping fence post
Standing here at the dam, I must imagine the soft calls

the cows make as they hurry across the ridge,
ears pricking at his voice, the call he makes just for them.
"Sue calves," he calls. "Sue calves."
They answer in their own secret way.
It is the way cows always speak.
"We love you," they say. "We love you."

Flag Run Ridge

Moonrise calls for kneeling.
Oh, I know.
But good Lord, the darkness
split open this way by a rising cuticle of light
breaking across the hill,
turning the apple trees to creatures
clawing the sky. That's a picture
asking for prayer.

I'm here on full moons, too,
but full moons have enough said,
in praise and fear, of them.
I'm praying to the lonely sickle.
It cuts the deep in me, turns
breathing to self-indulgence,
until I hold my breath in honor,
wish I could stop the heart that thumps
and thumps — I can wait. I can wait here.

I can wait until the moon turns
itself over again, until dark
covers the ridge altogether, a bath
crafted, somehow, by shame.

They say enough moonlight
makes a girl cycle with the phases.
I can wait that long. I can follow
both lightness and dark.

AFTER

The man waited for her. He waited
in the dark corners of his house,
where the dog came to find him, cold nose
against arm, rib. He waited
on the porch, scraping away
at the chipped, lead paint
with his thumbnail. In the crawl
space, with his knees in damp clay
and his head against cinder blocks,
mud crumbling into his hair.
In the attic corners strung
with web and fur, he settled in.
He sat there hunched
keeping an eye on her bicycle.
She will come, he thought, when that shadow
reaches the fifteenth spoke.

SLAB TOWN ROAD:
JACK'S DEFEAT CREEK

You were telling me about the river
and how you found the body.
You were about to say how the skin
stretched over her ankles, wilted along her chin,
came to a strange, yellow point
at the crown of her bald skull.
How the carp sucked the hair from her scalp,
how their must have been a feast
on the meat of her toes.

But I wanted the story of the dark slab
of ice you skated those winters, the story
of water sliding down your belly
after summer baths. I wanted the song
you sang late, when the catfish held out,
watching the hunched silhouette of your shoulders
on the bank. I wanted, even, the day
your father, red-faced and boiling, threw
you toward the reeling current, screamed
after your white stick arms.

But you wanted to tell the story of this woman.
And the wide holes in her face. You said,
She would have been so
beautiful if she were young.
You wanted to say she was the picture
of your sister, girl whose eyes
ride the same color as the river in fall: wide and deep and
turning. You told stories that came, swimming,
from no one's mouth but your own.

OXBOW
for D.

I saw a Cooper's Hawk drown a song sparrow,
calm as the day is long, in the oxbow
sluicing up north of here. The hawk
didn't mind me watching.
She just held her ground.

I reckon I've seen a thousand
deaths between the beginning and
the end of acres in this valley,
river bottom carved from old hills, a bowl
to catch the sky poured out from whoever holds
the pitcher (whoever does the pouring), river bottom
that taught me looking up shows us gunmetal
wings, flash of sky, flash of belly,
the danger that comes with the pouring.

Sick

My friend tells me his dad is sick.
My own coughs up blood every morning —
I could barely stand to sleep on his couch
last Christmas for the deep hurt
growing out of him. But he is mine,
and I know how to talk around the lung.
My friend set out today to visit his father,
a man bound for liver surgery. A liver removal and
replacement — a kind of carving.
I call a man I know who can tell
me about blood cell manufacturing
and the spleen and bile. I can't really hear —
voices filter in from outside.
He says today he gave the dog a bath.
As if the burrowing pain could be cleaned
and combed and curried into soap.
As if, on this day,
I remembered he had a dog at all.

SHUCKING CORN

August dusk. I was twelve, shucking corn
with Brother on our side porch.
Four rake-ribbed dogs trotted across our back
field, sweet saucer of green the two
of us, Brother and I, bush-hogged the day before. The dogs
bit at each other's tails. The big one, the red

one, lifted his head opened his red mouth yawned his red
yawn. When Daddy saw he threw corn
husks like arrows, high and pelting, until the dogs
ran hard for the woods — Brother, rooted to the porch
steps, watched the arc of field until two
red ears stopped, tipped, turned back.

The dog shook inside his skin, licked the back
of one paw, and howled at the sky. Red
boiling sky. Daddy shook his fist, said, "Don't you two
feed it." We could only carry our corn
in brown bags to the kitchen counter. We left the porch.
Left the fading sky, field of dogs.

But I've seen other dogs. Other red dogs.
Ones that swallowed wind from backs
of pickup trucks, ones that slept under porches
or stretched along the back of a red
plaid couch in the junkyard. Dogs trapped in corn
cribs. Dogs running down train tracks. Two

dogs barking at a man wielding a stick, two
boys throwing stones at a one-eyed dog
in a livery stable. I've read a book: two pups carried home in a cor
meal sack on a boy's back.
And they all remain in the red
slick of my eyes. If I fall asleep on the porch

swing, they come and curl on the porch
steps beneath me. They come two by two —
like Noah lives here, like it was Noah called the red
dog into our field, like it's Noah singing the dog
song until every man turns his head back
to this place. These fields, these dogs, this corn.

Brother waited two days on the porch steps
for the red dog's return. My father waits there still, looking
back to where corn grew on every side, when we,
     all of us, were small.

CAPTINA CREEK CULVERT

In this thing called moving
she discovered a way
of un-remembering.
She wears her bluejeans
with a new wide belt, name
tooled across the back.
She does not call
her father on his birthday.
She slouches,
wears her hair in a braid
that flies and folds and will not
be unbraided.
She makes a new name:
Radar and Counselor and Shame.
The lines of her mouth pull in.
Her whole face is smaller
than before.

A gar fans the sand, dropping eggs.
The fish tilts her eyes, shows
a snout so fine it could be pearl.
Dangerous things, these that
catch the light, full of grace.
The cold of river water cracks
itself against our girl's joints.
Silt so fine it shines against her skin — new
kind of fur. The creeping-up
bottom, the mud edging over her ankles,
stones bumping her shins.
There's the light sending a curve
down the Captina's spine, through the rise,

against the belly of the gar.
This river moves its way
behind her knees, up over the belt,
into her mouth when she crouches
to see the fish without the bent light.

No one remembers what she said
about family or her brother's new wife, only
that things were, in fact, said and that she
laughed with her hand over her mouth.
They see her standing up to her waist.
They see her kneeling.
They think — This is emergency.

STUMP TOWN ROAD
for P.

On the new moon, we come to lay down promises:

— to empty the shell on the shelf,
  wash the sand and snail
  from each little whirl.

— to dance when light wakes us again,
  touching the spot where you first
  kissed, where the cat came to die
  by the window, where white-crowned sparrows
  squabble at the feeder.

— to remember the tiny tides in our blood,
  the turning of that red stream like the curling
  of the waves on Pea Island, where sunrise always
  brought rain but nights burned
  clear, that sky a black and speckled bell
  domed over our beds.

We bring promises of lightning storms
yellowing the eastern sky, pulsing
over the hillside of prairie out your window.
Promises of gardens still blooming in fall.
Kale, red potatoes, squash in every color.
We promise hillbilly music.
We promise big dogs curled by little fires.
We promise sea salt and olives and black-eyed susans
pressed between the pages of a blue book.

Even Venus promises her heart as the morning star.

We will watch the bell-sky's slow progress
from this kitchen, where we gather to peer
toward the equinox, the balance of light that comes
after our dark night spent together, spent
in celebration. Spent in silence and joy at each little birth.

How to Run Away

Your belt fallen on the armchair.
I've thought maybe I should pick it up —
clutter doesn't matter anymore. Walking
home, eating tortillas
with our sweatshirt hoods
swept up around our necks,
oak tree full of crows, crows calling, the alley
leading down the hill to the river.

That river's where I first saw the scar
wrapping clear around your calf.
I wanted to taste you then.

When we walk home this way, I think
riverbanks are better suited in the pine grove
close to Reelsville, where I noodled channel cats
from logs til my forearms bled.
The '74 Chevy pickup that hashed the north shore
against the April current. Seining for minnows,
red flash of clay just below the sand.
I caught a gar once there, his snout plugged
up against my palm when I unsnagged the hook.

I heard Captina in the sewage culvert today —
you're welcome to come along. I can't help but go.

ORCHARD

The old farmers breakfast at Boone-Hutch Farm,
then walk the lower pastures, reckoning if this woven wire
will hold a herd of goats. When the weeping cherry
starts to bloom, the apple blossoms flush out.
I walk alone through our orchards. Last year
in a drought so vicious the bees got thirsty and drowned
themselves in the quarter inch of scum
still hiding along the bottom of the rain barrel, we lost
most every apple that blossomed.
Drout. Drought. Draught.
Wind or water, seeping this way or that,
draws the old farmers along the fencerows,
looking and looking — a little sign of corn
not washed or baked away.

CAT HOLLOW
for M.

Buried in leafmeal, skulls pock the woods
between your house and mine.

Two deer, a raccoon, fox kit, possum.
Little dog with the blue collar rotting, too.

Sunday mornings I walk head down
looking to find just one more —

a small offering. I arrive at your fencerow
before even the hens wake to scrabble

over the cantaloupe rind left from their dinner.
You sit on the porch steps with coffee,
squinting into the early sun, wrists on knees.

The woods between your house and mine
shelter more than what we find.

They give the distance between us a name,
lay down a ley line that burns and burns,

draws me back again each quiet Sunday
identifying cardinal flower and larkspur as I walk,

learning names so I can show you I know just
who lives here, in the miles between us.

Moving Heavy Things

I. Braking

From the yellow house to the little house,
warm windows to porch light powered by extension cord.
I take the dog with me, her blue eye flashing out at raccoons
pushing their little hands into the compost pile, her brown eye
tracking me, my course through the garden, past
green bell peppers, black in this dark light
hanging their weight from such small stems.

II. Tightening

Here is the hot twist of cotton into fist.
You keep imitating a crocus. Every morning
your hands turn white in the root
birth. I have this pile of shingles, plus
a barn side needs repair. The overlapping
tightens our grip most of all. The watertight
cedar helps us become lovers
of heft — the anvil your brother found
buried in the pig sty, the millstone you made into a table
in the back yard. Heavy things, they keep us.
It's the tightening of our fingers, and I'm thankful for the labor.

III. Wringing Down

I am the level platform built in the north meadow.
I am the plumb corner of a barn eve.
I am the dark painted elm limb,
blackened with tar, used as a club.

IV. Swigging

I've learned to lean out hard. The motion
bends the body to it, is the silent show
of how a ball and socket works, the slow
roll of one surface against and inside another.

CHAPEL

You didn't think she'd be this tall.
You didn't think her legs would move like cloud
shadows over a fallow field. But there she is.
Her lines have straightened, planed themselves
into shelves and mesas. You can see
how she has always been beautiful.
Always been growing.
Shame on you for not believing.

PORCH RAIL:
SISTER RETURNS HIS CALLS

Some days our blue porch
shines brighter in shadow.
I missed your phone calls —
4 times this month alone.
Don't forget to walk
your bird dog
when you get home.
Don't forget the night you said
I'd be ice-fishing
in the next year, holding
a pike so heavy with eggs
her mouth would seem too small
to feed them all. You said
you had a dream of hardwood floors
and a basketball
bouncing out the window.
Okay then. Okay.
But here is my new house
full of these men,
this one who stays close
even in cold, May rain.
Okay. I'm fishing
the spring river.
I'm full-blooded every time
I reel myself in.

Sandy Ridge Road

In the last of the rainy season, you are born
a kestrel seeking woodpecker holes. Your black barred
tail, your white face. The black stripes
show just how sad you might have been.
You keep flying over the road —
I keep wrecking my car.
When you perch up in the tulip poplar,
dark bird on a dark branch,
remember that we remember
you were born. And we remember
loving you, little bird. We remember
all the things you say.

Horse Barn: A Wedding
for C&C

In Ancient Egypt, carvers learned to use acacia and willow
to fit tight little dove tails. They saw beauty in trees that grew
close to home. I think love is like that. I think you are like that,
too, growing up in little ways so particular to how you grow.

My father hung a Frisbee swing in the silver maple in the back yard.
In Oregon, it was a copper beech planted
when the collie dog was just a pup. Here in the East,
an apple tree dropped its fruit for one little girl to gather.
What trees those were. What beautiful laughs our fathers have.
I imagine them newly born — small. And fragile. Think
of all things in their infancy, all of us, just born, just learning to hear
the world without the warble of liquid turning every word to song.

We have all gotten so tall. To start out, to be a little beech seed —
what must it have been like to be all of us, growing. To send out
one root here, one there. To reach east, to touch gently the root
of the dying pine where that little girl first learned to climb, first
learned to settle back against the trunk and read into dusk.

Here is what I mean to say:
This barn, this wind combing our hair, this gathering of people.
The carvers got it right. So did we. We're mitered
      all along our seams.

CPSIA information can be obtained at www.ICGtesting.com
Printed in the USA
LVOW06s2114211213

366366LV00002B/585/P

9 781625 490599